Love Letters To Myself

Hylain Rackley

BookLeaf Publishing

India | USA | UK

Presentation by *BookLeaf Publishing*

Web: www.bookleafpub.com

E-mail: info@bookleafpub.com

ISBN: 9789358737332

First edition 2023

I dedicate this book to my loves:

Ryan, Claudia and Emily.

And to all of you who have been there for me to cheer me on.

Thank you.

ACKNOWLEDGEMENT

Thank you Bookleaf Publishing for giving me the opportunity to articulate my thoughts on paper and for my art to be out there in the world to be shared and discovered.

I never thought my first book Simple Joys would have been received as well as it has and I am so grateful for everyone who has show me support as an author.

Thank you to all my friends and family for all the ongoing support and praise for my artistic endeavors.

PREFACE

With so much negativity in the news and talk about depression and anxiety all around us like it is the new normal, it is time to focus on positive things that are happening all around us and look within ourselves to find a sense of empowerment and a level of self-love to feel happy.

This haiku poetry book offers short stories about what is there right now to help you find that inner peace.

Use your own imagination to make the positive imagery come to live and feel the positive energy life has to offer.

Enjoy Love Letters To Myself.

Be present

Right now you are here
Live each day to the fullest
The time flies, tick tock

Stay positive

Allow yourself thoughts
Journal and unlock pure bliss
Positive mindset

Create your own universe

Galaxies are made
by collapsing and burning
Don't apologize

Love letters

Please write love letters
Full of grace and gratitude
To yourself daily

Pillow talk

5

My head rests softly
Comfortably close to yours
Let us share our dreams

Bloom where you are planted

A seed in the dark
A bud waiting to explode
A blooming flower

Goddess mode

Smile like you mean it
Nourish your inner goddess
You are beautiful

Grounded

Barefoot on the grass
Create your own paradise
Feel grounded right here

Family

You watched me grow up
I keep you close to my heart
You made me myself

Pampering time

You fix everything
Magic happens on my back
When your fingers touch

Cardinals

Do you believe that
Those with red feathers watch us?
They left but stayed near

Man's best friend

Questioning big eyes
Always loyal always there
Your head on my lap

Sweater weather

Sky high moving clouds
Howling storm with gusts of wind
Wear a warm sweater

A warm beverage

Steeped herbal delight
Or a steaming cup of milk
Enjoy a cuppa

Mindful art

Slowly making art
Rhythmic ticking of needles
One row at the time

Ripple effect

In sync left to right
Soft ripples in the water
The flow of nature

Dreams of Paris

Mon cœur mon amour
Imagination is key
Fly away with me

Picture perfect

Do you feel wholesome
When the sun makes your skin glow?
Capture the moment

Bonfire

Flannel pajamas
Gather around the bonfire
Let's enjoy charred s'mores

Rain

Trickling down slowly
Rainy days bring out comfort
Happy to be home

Take action

Inspire your mind
Please chase what makes you happy
Go live your best life